Greg Delanty was born in Cork in 1958. He was educated at University College Cork, where he obtained a BA in English and History in 1980, and a Higher Diploma in Education in 1982. He was the visiting poet at the University of Vermont in 1986 and at New York University in the summer of 1991. He was poet in residence at the Frost Place, Franconia, in 1988. Since 1987 he has been a lecturer at St Michael's College, Vermont. His work has appeared in numerous newspapers and journals, including the *Atlantic Monthly*, the *Irish Review*, the *Los Angeles Times*, the *Times Literary Supplement*, the *Irish Times* and the *Boston Herald*. In 1983 he was presented with the Patrick Kavanagh Award and in 1986 he was awarded the Allan Dowling Poetry Fellowship. His previous collections are *Cast in the Fire* (1986) and *Southward* (1992); with Nuala Ní Dhomhnaill he has edited an anthology of poetry, *Jumping Off Shadows: Selected Contemporary Irish Poets* (1995).

D1048804

american wake

greg delanty

THE
BLACKSTAFF
PRESS

BELFAST

HOUSTON PUBLIC LIBRARY

R01031 30388

HUMCA

First published in 1995 by
The Blackstaff Press Limited
3 Galway Park, Dundonald, Belfast BT16 0AN, Northern Ireland
with the assistance of
The Arts Council of Northern Ireland

Reprinted 1996

© Greg Delanty, 1995
All rights reserved

Typeset by Paragon Typesetters, Queensferry, Clwyd

Printed in Ireland by ColourBooks Limited

A CIP catalogue record for this book
is available from the British Library

ISBN 0-85640-549-3

ACKNOWLEDGEMENTS

Some of these poems have previously appeared in *Antioch Review*, *Boston Herald*, *College English*, *Decentralisation of Government* (DOCAL), *Éire–Ireland*, *Fortnight*, *Green Mountains Review*, *Irish Poetry Now* (Wolfhound Press), *Irish Times*, *Jumping Off Shadows: Selected Contemporary Irish Poets* (Cork University Press), *London Magazine*, *Meanjin*, *New Myths*, *New Republic*, *New Statesman*, *New Virginia Review*, *Pivot*, *Poetry Ireland*, *Prairie Schooner*, and *Southern Review*, and have been broadcast on RTE television and radio. 'After Viewing *The Bowling Match at Castlemary, Cloyne 1847*' appeared in the *Atlantic Monthly* in February 1995.

'After Viewing *The Bowling Match at Castlemary, Cloyne 1847*' was written to Katie Conboy, Tom O'Grady, and John Engels.

'The Heritage Centre, Cobh 1993' was written to Catherine Coakley and Thomas McCarthy.

'*Economic Pressure*' was written especially for the Reverend Joseph McLoughlin.

'In Search of the American Celts' was written to Erica Kamins and Nick Farrell.

'Searching for a Gift' was a wedding present to Sandra Good and Rory Lehane.

Many people helped me with the preparation of this book. I would like to thank them and St Michael's College, Vermont.

May your words unfold
   like the comforting wings
of Fionnuala, sheltering
   her exiled siblings,
cursed with a magic song
   no one hears them sing;
of their exile this is
   the cruellest of suffering.

CONTENTS

PROEM

The Fifth Province   3

PART I

After Viewing *The Bowling Match at Castlemary,*
    Cloyne 1847   7
The Heritage Centre, Cobh 1993   8
Christopher Ricks's Oxford   9
The Fat Yank's Lament   11
To President Mary Robinson   12
Economic Pressure   13
Tracks of the Ancestors   15
In the Land of the Eagle   17
America   18
In Search of the American Celts   19
Vermont Aisling   20

PART II

On the Renovation of Ellis Island   23
The Gift   24
Sin Street   25
Backfire   26
Developing the Negative   27
Searching for a Gift   28
According to the Horticulturist, it is Unlikely Our
    Fuchsia will Survive the Winter   29

PART III

Though the World is Gone Mad   33
The Cove   34
Keeping Distance   35

While Reading *Poets in their Youth*   36
Prospecting on Abbey Island   37
At a Low Point   38
To Some Friends   39
On the Marriage of Friends   40
The Shrinking World   41

PART IV

The Splinters   45

ENVOY

The Children of Lir   61

PROEM

THE FIFTH PROVINCE

Meeting in a café, we shun the cliché of a pub.
    Your sometime Jackeen accent is decaffed
like our coffee, insisting you're still a Dub.
    You kid about being half & halfed.
The people populating your dreams are now
    American, though the country they're set in
    is always the Ireland within a soft Dublin.

In the country of sleep the voiceless citizens
    trapped in my regime of dreams are Irish,
but they're all the unlikely green denizens
    of an island that's as mysterious
as the volcano, bird or sheep islands
    that Brendan with his homesick crew,
    bound for the Promised Land, bumped into.

Last night I combed sleep's shore for its name.
    A familiar adze-crowned man appeared
waving his crook's question mark, nursing a flame
    on a hill and impatiently declaring in weird
pidgin Irish that the fifth province is
    not Meath or the Hy Brasil of the mind.
    It is this island where all exiles naturally land.

PART I

In them uncover the destiny
    of everyone,
for all are exiled & in search
    of a home,
as you settle the eroding
    island of each poem.

AFTER VIEWING *THE BOWLING MATCH AT CASTLEMARY, CLOYNE 1847*

I promised to show you the bowlers
   out the Blarney Road after Sunday mass,
you were so taken with that painting
   of the snazzy, top-hatted peasant class
     all agog at the bowler in full swing,
     down to his open shirt, in trousers
as indecently tight as a baseballer's.

You would relish each fling's span
   along blackberry boreens, and delight
in a dinger of a curve throw
   as the bowl hurls out of sight,
     not to mention the earthy lingo
     & antics of gambling fans,
giving players thumbs-up or down the banks.

It's not just to witness such shenanigans
   for themselves, but to be relieved
from whatever lurks in our background,
   just as the picture's crowd is freed
     of famine & exile darkening the land,
     waiting to see where the bowl spins
off, a planet out of orbit, and who wins.

7

THE HERITAGE CENTRE, COBH 1993

The Cobh train might be a time machine
transporting us from the smog-shrouded city.
Chemical plants surrounding the Lee
& harbour flick by into the future.
We enter the simulated coffin ship
& peruse dioramas of papier-mâché emigrants
poised in various stages of travail,
accompanied by the canned clamour
of goodbyes, hooters, & sailors rigging mast.

We are back doing Lent's Stations
from convict ship to the grand finale
of the *Lusitania* & *Titanic*, buried
in the sea's unopened sepulchre.
The *Titanic*'s washed-up spyglass
is too rusted to extend further.
Turned the wrong way around,
everything diminishes & goes far off

just as our own island goes further
from what we want each day: a place
no one has to leave for another land.
But I keep doomsaying theatrics to myself,
afraid I'd sound like that diver's commentary,
down for the first televised time in the *Titanic*,
dramatising the merest chink at every stage,
from first-class cabins, below to the dark,
fathomless eternity of the gashed steerage.

8

CHRISTOPHER RICKS'S OXFORD

Meeting in your old stomping ground,
you led me through the arch to another era.
The walls excluded vulgar traffic sound
& the quad's limestone was suitably sepia.

It all seemed a parody of English
order & monocled high seriousness,
but then wasn't I a parody of the Irish
with my hangover & rebellious

inferiority, or was it superiority?
Both, perhaps. The cultured fuchsia
flourishing in floral regiments made me
feel as alien as back in America.

I'd just left behind the weeping, wild
fuchsia that bedecked & defined Derrynane,
having returned from the still new New World
to a home that's restricted now to vacation.

I think the sinister English order undid me,
or rather the monstrous, dark disorder
it pretends to control so assuredly,
as if somehow darkness can be checked for ever.

Yet look, I rally & order each word
in an English drill especially for you

who seemed most at home in Oxford,
since I know order is all we have to subdue

darkness, inevitable as the snow of New England,
where we both settle now, attempting home,
and since where I'm from in Ireland
home is a full rhyme with single-syllabled *poem*.

THE FAT YANK'S LAMENT
to the Irish-Irish

How were any of us wiseguy kids to know
when we mocked busloads of rotund Yanks
bleating WOW! along every hedgerow
from Malin Head down to the Lee banks,
searching for the needle in the haystack
of ancestors with names like Muh-hone-ey
or Don-a-hue,
                that I'd one day come back
a returned Yank myself, & you'd mock me
when I let slip restroom or gas station.
You accuse me of scoffing too many hot dogs,
siding unwittingly with my Vermont physician.
Now I'm even considering daily jogs,
concerned not so much for my unhealthy state,
but the scales of your eyes reading my weight.

TO PRESIDENT MARY ROBINSON

Yes, we're moved by the light in your window
    but, returning on another brief holiday
    from England, Australia or the USA,
we can't help feel somewhat mocked by its glow.
For though we know full well we are no
    Holy Family, we're still turned away
    to settle in the unfamiliar, cold hay.

ECONOMIC PRESSURE

I traipsed beneath pictures
week in week out, an urchin,
on my reluctant way upstairs
to Mr Murphy's art class.
I liked *Time Flies*, *The Falconer*,
View of Cork, *The Fiddler*,
The Bowler, *The Boxer*,
but most of all *Men of the South* –
I suppose because of the guns
& the idea of heroism
& the good & bad guys
& the 1916 anniversary
& all that hullabaloo.
But I never bothered much
with that emigration canvas.
I may even have ignored it
the way I snubbed the lasher
of our class, Kathleen whatshername,
just to show I honestly
didn't care a fig for her.
But today at the departure
gate of the airport
it finally caught up with me.
I saw again the woman
with her head buried
in the near shoulder
of her black-coated
son or husband.
Two men are turned away,

13

out of politeness,
embarrassment, or both.
One leans beneath
a scrawny tree that struggles,
like any immigrant,
in strange rock.
The other, with his back to us,
perhaps hides despair at yet
another leaving the picture.
The currach suggests
the anxiety of them all
to put the scene behind.
Its bow is aimed
away from the island's past,
out to a boat
with its sail at half mast.

TRACKS OF THE ANCESTORS
to Louis de Paor

Along a boreen of bumblebees,
    blackahs & fuchsia,
somewhere around Dunquin,
    you said that Pangaea

split there first & America
    drifted away from Kerry
& anyone standing on the crack
    got torn in two slowly.

We never dreamed we'd end up
    on other continents,
hankering for familiar mountains,
    rivers & grey firmament.

Out where you've settled,
    the Aborigines
recite dreamtime songs
    that signpost journeys.

The shifting of each verse
    directs which way to go,
celebrating rainbow serpent
    & sky hero.

As we traverse our landscapes,
    whether city, prairie,

bush or bog, we are
    walkabout Aborigine.

We can't identify where
    exactly we are from day to day,
but if we hold to songlines
    we shouldn't go astray.

IN THE LAND OF THE EAGLE

Our first night here we pubcrawled
the Bronx, still too new
for us not to be enthralled
by the street life & brew

of all-night watering holes
with names like The Shamrock
or Galway Shawl, full of legals
& illegals longing to go back,

lowering pint after pint
of their staggering Irishness,
sláinte-ing the Dubs' winning point,
cursing American Guinness . . .

After that country for old men
abandoned them like the gannet
abandons its fledgling,
not all of them make it.

Those that do are more
like the wren who flew high
off the eagle of folklore,
prevailing in the contentious sky.

AMERICA

I'm buffaloed
by this landscape
without voice
or memory.

Perhaps it powwows
with surviving Abenaki
the way Iveragh or Beara
parleys with us.

Yet I can't help but feel
like one of Brendan's crew,
oblivious to the nature
of the fishy shore

they settled
before the whale
beneath their feet
surged to life.

IN SEARCH OF THE AMERICAN CELTS

It was less far-fetched for you that Bran
or Brendan or some other Celt actually
built those stone chambers through New England,
but I tagged along for the company.

As we drove through Vermont's annual ice age,
you remarked that the extinction of Celts here
was as sudden, but not as strange,
as the disappearance of dinosaurs.

We tailed the mountain road as far as snow
would allow & then stepped from the road's shore
into the unknown snow depths of the meadow,
as if negotiating an unfamiliar river floor.

I had prepared myself to pretend to be
impressed, but I wasn't putting you on
when I swore we could be in the old country,
boggled by this ruin aligned with December's sun.

Inside the lintel I got the notion
we would walk back out to Derrynane fuchsia
jigging above the jagged Kerry ocean.
I shunned the wiles of nostalgia,

knowing if anyone could step inside me
they'd end up in this chamber with its row
of fading carvings to some Celtic deity,
but on walking out they'd find nothing but snow.

VERMONT AISLING

Vermont was like a wooer
whose attraction
you shut out, preoccupied
with a lifelong crush.

But lately
you've been taken
with this place,
especially since

snow covers
any resemblance
to that other one
& its perpetual row,

stilled beneath
the snow's silence.
May it snow for ever
& for ever now.

PART II

Had shed blood been ink, I could still be
quilling *The Faerie Queene*, but I did not
allow a drop to blot a mere sonnet
that you, trapped in complicity, can never
quite break free of. Admit it, hypocrite!

ON THE RENOVATION OF ELLIS ISLAND

What is even worse than if the walls wept
like a mythical character trapped in wood
or stone is that the walls give off nothing:
nothing of all those who were chalk-branded
for a limp, bedraggled look or vacant brow;
nothing of the man who thought Liberty
wore a crown of thorns; nothing of boys
who believed that each foot of anyone
who wore pointed shoes had only one toe;
nothing of mothers clutching tattered shawls
& belt-strapped cases like Old World beliefs;
nothing of petticoated women who turned flapper . . .
Surely if we stripped the coats of fresh paint
as anxiously as those women undid petticoats,
walls would weep, but for nothing now, for ever.

THE GIFT

*to two emigrants, Orlaith & Gerry, who returned to Ireland to
be married*

It rained cats & dogs all day on your day,
the day you'll open up in an album
back on Broadway & sentimental eyes will stray
over this snap or that: of a sozzled chum
after a stave, bellising his noble call;
aunts connishuring under umbrellas & confetti;
uncles promising to take the tack after it all;
you knowing you're poxed despite the pawny,
laughing at the razzing behind a camera
or slagging characters you've not seen in yonks,
as photos curl in dog days of America
and you curse the sleepless, humid Bronx,
wishing for your wedding day gift of rain –
its absence a dry, out–of–the–blue pain.

SIN STREET

Again you are drawn to neon-lit Sin Street,
pretending to be at your cool-dude ease.
Prostitutes, pimps & pushers patrol their beat.
You join other men as driven as drone bees
swarming the files of peepshow confessionals.
Shutters open to the mind's X-rated movies
and fumbling, solitary men sacrifice themselves
to their bodies, as committed as those braves
who carnally submit themselves to be reborn.
Afterwards guilt ravishes you as you flee
this underworld of eternal crys & groans
beckoning behind each door's bolted fantasy.
Men struggle in the quicksand of lust,
longing to rest in the coming dust.

BACKFIRE
4 July 1991

You recall how fireworks were invented
to ward off evil, as they rise high
above the Milky Way of Manhattan.

They form into blue, red & white stars
floating in brief constellations,
then scatter like blown dandelions.

Loudspeakers welcome back soldiers,
who plug their gas pump salutes
to their foreheads as generals cruise by.

Victory dismisses all who died.
Fireworks turn into flares for help
among the bustle & boom of bombardment.

One blossoms into a weeping willow & hangs
above skyscrapers rising like tombstones.

DEVELOPING THE NEGATIVE

On not being allowed to sign a petition banning
pornography because I am male

The petitioning woman brandished a poster
that declared: NATIVE AMERICANS ARE RIGHT –
THE CAMERA STEALS THE SOULS OF ALL TAKEN.
After she spurned & turned me away I mull
over all I should have said, always dumb
at the spur of the hot-blooded moment.
How if I could I'd crack open every Kodak,
Canon, Olympus, right down to those primitive
leg-spread contraptions with curtains
that the taker peered through like a voyeur.
I would scurry about, giving each soul back.
Instead I stumble down the accusing street,
confused by the surprise snap of her eyes
that caught me with their blinding flash.

SEARCHING FOR A GIFT

I shanksmare down Broadway past Times Square
& try not to look unnerved by hustlers
– the way I would passing a growling dog –
knowing they'll close in if they sense
I'm on edge. Above us the news relays
chosen minute–by–minute disasters:
CNN generals nod football–big heads,
praising a patriot's interception
& the blazing shot of accurate missiles.
Then, in the sudden luckybag way things happen
in Manhattan, a baglady with a face as wrinkled
as the shawlie fruitseller at Tralee Market
hands me something I'd like to give you:
a bunch of Derrynane blue hydrangea.

ACCORDING TO THE HORTICULTURIST, IT IS UNLIKELY OUR FUCHSIA WILL SURVIVE THE WINTER

When friends mused that literature was more
than likely kaput, our fuchsia came to mind.
Not of August's billowing plant
bought on our return from babbling Manhattan,
but of it pruned to stumpy, bare branches
in the hope of blossom next summer.
We have taken it back inside & set the pot
in the most light-enamoured window.
Regularly before bed it is watered
as the silence of snow gathers outside,
covering the stiff body of the earth.
Drops form on the tips of amputated stems,
in search of phantom limbs & flowers.
They could be tears for the dead, or buds.

PART III

as the hermit crab & sea anemone
are dependent on one another

THOUGH THE WORLD IS GONE MAD

The gold coin of the sun
slips into the slot
of a mountain gap
& out comes a full moon
that is more golden than pale.

It's as if the coin has dropped
in us & we can hear again
the music of everything.
A heron rises clapping its wings.
A yacht nods *yes*.

And *yes* especially now
we're loafing up to Bridie's
that's more a shebeen than a pub,
loud with glorious banter
& talk about nothing.

If someone manoeuvres a singsong,
I would like to recite
something with the calming sway
of the slumbering sea
& the breeze massaging us

with honeysuckle, stout,
& the laughter of old friends
guffawing from the pub
to banish the thought of how
the music will soon play out.

THE COVE

Now I find peace in everything around me;
in the modest campion & the shoals of light
leaping across the swaying sea
& the gulls gliding out of sight.
The tops of wave-confettied rocks
slide into water & turn into seals.
They move to the lively reel
of the cove's clapping dance hall,
raising blithe yelps above the sea's music.
The ocean draws in & out like an accordion
& unseen lithe fingers play the strings
of joy on what the moment brings.
The seals close & part & close again.
Their awkward fins have turned to wings.

KEEPING DISTANCE

The ground's still too damp,
but we find a rocky patch to
perch on. Black & white ducks
surfacedive toward us.
From the woods across
the cove a moose bellows.
A woodpecker drills
& an oriole broadcasts.
Human voices sound far off.
There is so much sweetness
in distance. The sun reflects
in the water below us.
The murkiness of the lake
after winter's sudden thaw
veils its shimmer
and turns the sun in the water
into the moon. Now I know what
the ducks are diving for –
I'll never again think Li Po,
tippling, drowned foolishly.

WHILE READING *POETS IN THEIR YOUTH*

Reading by candle in the caravan
I'm disturbed by a moth fluttering
around my book & then the flame.
It drops with a waxen, burning smell
that reminds me of Icarus & Daedalus;
how I used to get the two confused
& how I've always wanted to know why
exactly moths are drawn to light;
why starlings batter themselves
at lighthouses & what safeguards
there are for those who fly by night.

PROSPECTING ON ABBEY ISLAND

I'd like to say that the treasure hunters,
obsessively hoovering the quiet strand
with their unresponsive metal detectors,
should raise their heads from the sand
& discover the treasure of the doubloon sun;
the pearl gulls above the waves;
the arrow showers of mackerel on the run;
the sea surging into shimmering caves
& laying out necklace shells & starfish
on the strand's gold carpet . . .
                                  But now this treasure
isn't enough & I wish that I did not wish
I wanted something beyond this measure
of what normally suffices & gives peace.
What exactly I want I can't exactly say.
Perhaps it is a more permanent release
from the flotsam of trouble washed up each day.
Whatever it is seems less detectable
than finding a gold piece in sand or shingle.

AT A LOW POINT

Grounded boats bask on their sides
as men lean on the pint-settling counter,
having rowed in with the flood tide.

Hermit crabs retreat to their cells
of empty whelk shells over
closing black & blue mussels.

Beached, blistered bladderwrack
drapes barnacled rocks
that hide periwinkle in every crack.

Lugworm serve up spaghetti mounds of sand
as they urgently burrow for cover,
evading even the angler's hand.

Now it's time to outwit such a reach
& learn the ways of the sea shore
as ebb tide's curtain lifts along the beach.

TO SOME FRIENDS

I have taken being ditched by lovers
& know that the owl, bullfinch, crow & swan
are among the few couples that stay partners.

But it is difficult to take
your silence when even migrating geese
honk to stay together & long-tailed tits make

twittering keep-in-touch calls among trees.
And oh, how we honked & how we twittered.
And when anyone was in trouble

the rest whistled around like a dolphin pod,
helped them to the surface on the double
& protected them against the predator.

It's said the dolphin's grin has nothing to do
with happiness, but enables one to hear
the other's song. My grin strains to hear you.

ON THE MARRIAGE OF FRIENDS

So you have chosen the way of the swan;
the way, perhaps, that is not natural
to everyone, but I will not harp on
about heron, bluebird or dotterel,

nor how the male flycatcher pairs
with two females, keeping a mile between,
so neither cops how the other shares
the same philandering gentleman.

Did you know the life-coupling way
of the swan is also that of the crow?
And there'll be crow-black days
you'll caw at each other with blind gusto.

But there'll be times when you'll sing
the duet of the black-collared barbet,
with the first part of the song sung
by one & the second by the mate.

We wish you now many such duet days
& sing for you like the red-eyed vireo
who sings nonstop through the summer blaze
on this day you take the way of swan & crow.

THE SHRINKING WORLD
to Mary & Niall on Catherine's first summer

Reading how the European long-tailed tit
builds a perfect domed nest, gathering lichen
for camouflage, feathers to line it
& cobwebs as binding so the nest can

stretch while chicks grow, I thought of you
rushing to crying Catherine, as if her mouth shone
like those of finchlings guiding parents through
darkness. If only chainsaw-armed men,

felling whole forests by the minute,
could have seen you hover around your fledgling,
they would have immediately cut
engines & listened to your lullabying.

But their lumbering motors drone on
in the distance & perhaps approach us.
And what about all those other Catherines,
imperial woodpeckers & birds of paradise?

I sing now like the North American brown thrasher,
who at one point in its song orchestrates
four different notes: one grieves, another
frets, a third prays, but a fourth celebrates.

PART IV

THE SPLINTERS

we ride the horses of Don –
although we are alive, we are dead!
from 'The Death Tale of Conaire'

I

The ferry furrows
the foam
of each lost century,
leaving a wake
that quickly settles
& forgets us,
as it has forgotten
all those who have
opened these waters:
fisherman, monk, pilgrim & pagan,
some foundering here.
Oisín with his beloved
flew on a winged horse
to Tír na nÓg this way,
waving goodbye
to the world he knew.
As our mainland
world diminishes,
there is respite.
A cloud engulfs us
out of nowhere
as if the miraculous
were about to appear.

The veil rises
to reveal the Small Skellig
& Skellig Michael
rising like chapel & cathedral.

II

We forget speech, hypnotised by the climb,
concentrating on narrow, rock-hewn steps
that spiral up like the symbolic gyres
of the Book of Kells, whorling in labyrinths
of knowledge, turmoil & eternity.
They lead to beehive huts & oratories
packed with a congregation of sightseers
who whisper in disbelief & reverence
at how those sometime monks lived
in this wind-tugged cloister of shells.

We browse in each dome's live absence
& picnic above the graveyard
that's no bigger than a currach
with a crucifix for helmsman,
navigating his crew to the island of the dead.
We're eyed by staunch, monkish puffins.
Our tongues loosen, but in keeping
with the sombreness of this sun-haloed place,
we chat about the world with an earnestness
that would embarrass us on the mainland.

You tell of how medieval monks charted world maps
with countries drawn as humans gorging upon
each other's entangled bodies. We go on to
the lands & demons of the worlds of love & poetry.

I'm flummoxed when you ask what poetry is.
I recall how the earliest musical instruments
were hewn out of bones, & that poets
carve their words out of those gone before.
They are the primitive musicians who beat
& blow words to life. More than that I do not know.

III

I lie in the sun,
my head in the shade
of a rock,
& doze above the ramparts
overlooking Teach Duinn.
Somehow we're ferrying
to these splintered islands once more,
tense beneath bellying canvas.
The keel parts
the seal-grey sea
& we wave to the shore.
An oneiric mist shrouds us
out of nowhere.
It vanishes as quickly.
We are here,
helping each other out
of the seesawing boat
with each uplift
of the sea's surge.
Our leaking picnic wine
turns into a libation
for the dead.
The figure of my father appears.
I reach to embrace him,

but clasp nothing.
I beseech him to drink.
He waves it away, knowing
I'll need the wine
to give voice to others
who can better guide me
& that words are not necessary
between us.
His form fades
& out of his figure
another emerges
who drinks the wine
& directs the way.
Another takes his place
& another.
They drink their fill
& say their say:

Amergin

    Sing of the birds' sunrise cacophony,
    discordant as any orchestra
    tuning up before the day's symphony.
    Sing of the flocks of waves riding in,
    delicately curved as a swan's neck.
    Sing of the sun's descent in tongues of fire
    upon the sea, communing with all & sundry.
    Sing of the smell of the ocean, sweeter
    than the scent of cut grass or girls;
    then sing of these, for nothing is lovelier.
    Sing of the broken mirror of the sea
    faithful to everything passing above.
    Sing of the sun pulling its own shroud over

the mirror & of how shearwater pierce the dark.
Sing of the tide-beckoning moon.
Sing of all you behold from sunrise to sunrise
& of how I'm within everything wherever you go.
Who am I? Only by singing will you know.

Cú Chulainn

If it's true that we view ourselves
    by our reflection in others' eyes
then I'd rush to a druidic shrink
    who'd admit me to a straitjacket cell,

since more than one of my multiple characters
    likes to bomb, kneecap & cause general hell.
One minute I'm potshotting pubcrawling amadáns
    of popery & the next I'm geligniting a bunch

of drum-pounding Orange gligíns sky high,
    not to speak of innocent passersby.
Untie me from the stake of your eyes
    and allow me a bit of shuteye.

The Old Woman of Beare

Please, do not recoil
    from my shrivelled face.
Sing of how my love & I
    passed our day on Skellig

long before the ebb tide
    of old age forced me

to grip the driftwood
　　of God's safer love.

We slipped from the climbing,
　　somnambulant pilgrimage
of bowed figures as they clasp
　　their chains of beads

& edged to an outcrop
　　along a narrow ledge
where kittiwakes could hardly
　　reed their nest of weeds.

We clasped each other's
　　trembling hands,
not so much from fear
　　of being caught

by the blackbacked priest
　　or falling
like wingless chicks,
　　but from a need to touch.

We entwined as tightly
　　as any intricate nest,
becoming our own nest
　　on reaching the rock spur.

We took it as a good omen
　　seeing the brace of seals
tossing the surf's lace,
　　soughing as if in pain.

But if it was pain,
 it was the relief
of undressing & balming
 a fresh wound.

Our unbecoming bodies
 became our very souls
& we & the sky & the water
 swayed timelessly in time

as he surged in & out
 like the waves below
filling & emptying
 dark, weeping caves.

Edmund Spenser

 That dusk at Dún an Óir we slaughtered even
the pregnant, whimpering women methodically
while a bloodstained sun drowned in the ocean.
Each foetus struggled in the belly
of each slain mother as desperately
as a lobster dropped in a boiling pot.
Had shed blood been ink, I could still be
quilling *The Faerie Queene*, but I did not
allow a drop to blot a mere sonnet
that you, trapped in complicity, can never
quite break free of. Admit it, hypocrite!
In your time few are not guilty of slaughter.
Even the page you'll pen this upon is of pine
that Amazonians were shot for. I could go on . . .

Aogán Ó Rathaille

I lifted the pitch of my grief
    above the storm-crashing waves
for my world breaking on the reefs
    of foreign, land-grabbing knaves.

But how can any *file* raise a plaint
    to match the world's Big House
being undone by absentee landlords
    of Wall Street & such dross.

They ignore dependence upon
    the lowliest plants & creatures
as the hermit crab & sea anemone
    are dependent on one another.

But no matter what, you must
    keen for all the world's theft
as I keened mine, despite knowing
    that soon no one may be left.

Eoghan Rua Ó Súilleabháin

Lend an ear to one of your own kind
    & do not let yourself be caught
by the winds of lust, like Dante's starlings
    blown this way & that by every gust.

I myself was borne on this wind
    as I whoremongered across the country,
always wary that around the next bend
    some ditched damsel would catch me.

My playboy life squandered energy
    that I should have instilled in song
more worthy of the muse-gift given to me
    than my occasional aisling.

Pay particular heed of me, especially
    since your word-talent is less than mine.
I'm still too bushed to eke out a last line.

Eibhlín Dubh Ní Chonaill
    Sing up front,
    cold-shouldering
    the fashionable
    low key of your time,
    closed, cautious & cute
    as a Kerry farmer.

    Sing as open-throated
    as my curlew-keen.
    I supped of Art's blood
    as he lay slain,
    already becoming Cork mud.

    Sing as full-throated
    as my unmatched plaint;
    matching my words
    to his cold body
    that would never again
    rouse to my touch.
    My hands wept
    that day's icy rain
    as I swore to undo

that kowtowing
dribble of a man
who slew my Art
of the wave-white horse.

The spirit of that mare
I rode
fleeter than any hare,
fleeter than any deer,
fleeter even than the wind
through Munster's open country.

Sing that elder
province of poetry.

Tomás Rua Ó Súilleabháin

I sang not for my own or beauty's sake
as much as to keep our spirits fired,
knowing as long as we sang we'd not break,
refusing to let the country be shired.
But it was too much when even our own land
turned hostile & drove us like lapwings
in hard winter, together in dying bands,
our swollen bellies pregnant with nothing.
Even the birds seemed to give up singing,
so I lay down & relinquished song.
But I should've kept up my amhrán-ing,
adapting & transmuting their tongue,
as your kind must now, keening everyone strong
by singing of & out of all the world's wrong.

Robin Flower

>Tell of those weather-sketched
> Attic islanders
>who half tamed their school
> of rocky Blaskets,
>water spouting from the blowholes
> of cliffs.

>Tell how they were forced
> from their Ithaca,
>still dreaming in the surf-rush
> of Irish,
>perpetually longing for the lilt
> of the sea.

>In them uncover the destiny
> of everyone,
>for all are exiled & in search
> of a home,
>as you settle the eroding
> island of each poem.

Austin Clarke

>Spenser was right, but if you're trapped
> in his sonnet's complicity like someone
>caught on the fourteen inaccessible steps
> mysteriously carved in the cliff
>that lead neither to sea nor to higher levels,
> then fashion them with your own hammer
> in the Gaelic manner, muffling rhyme.

>And since sonnets began amorous, to hell
> with the world's guilt, & tell of how such

55

& such a female's undulant breasts curve
    with your lust below a low-cut blouse;
how your owl-head gyroscopes on the street
    after others & how you stayed awake
    all night, illumined in another's light.

Patrick Kavanagh

The islands' standing army
of gannets fiercely snap,
stab & peck each other
or any creature who comes near,
but none could match
the terror I unleashed
on any who encroached
into my territory. I spat
abuse with petrel accuracy,
only far fouler than his spray.
I should have had the wisdom
of the sad-eyed puffins
who let everyone come close,
sensing that few mean hurt,
though when forced to tussle
they'll show their worth.
So learn from me,
but when I come to mind,
think not of how, brawling,
I knocked nests of words
over the edge,
splattering on the rocks
to the crude squawks of other
ravaging, wing-elbowing birds;
rather think of the winged poems

I hatched & how they're seen
regardless of time & place,
gliding & gyring
with their own certain grace.

Louis MacNeice
Life when it is gone is like a woman
you were glad to be quit of only to find
yourself years later longing for her
when you catch her scent on a packed street.
Tell me of the seagull plundering your picnic
before it wakes you. Tell me of rain
tapping a windowpane while you're ensconced
by the fire cradling the pregnant brandy glass.
Can you still hear a distant train blow?
Wet my whistle with a slug of Guinness.
What is the texture of fresh-fallen snow?
Do girls still wear their hair in braid?
What's tea? What's the smell of the sea?
Tell me. Tell me. I am beginning to fade.

IV

The alarming, silhouetted bird
has a preternatural quality
as it flutters around
my stirring head,
infiltrating my dream
& drawing me
from sleep's underworld,
rising with a scream.
I resist its pull.

Now everything turns
into dream's usual montage.
Another face emerges
but says nothing,
as if that's what he came to say.
His face turns into
one of a tongueless woman.
The face vanishes.
Dolphins break
beyond Blind Man's Cove,
returning the dead
to Bull Island,
broadcasting underwater song
whose timbre is the soul
of loneliness.
Now the ferryman informs us
that Skellig Michael
was once a druidic site.
His oil-wrinkled hands tug
the engine cord.
He coaxes our boat
out of the cliff-shaded cove,
opening a path
through the grape-green sea.
We withdraw
into the distance.
I wake
with the disgruntling knowledge
that we've touched only the tip
of these dark icebergs.

ENVOY